100 THINGS BLACK BOYS SHOULD DO AND KNOW

by Jason "NS" Huey

ISBN-13: 978-0-578-28821-5

Cover Design by Ebony Simpson

Editing by Kyle Marie McMahon of Literatus Editing & Prose

SHOUT-OUT

Mary Huey and Wilson Huey for birthing me. Tawana, Crystal, and Cricket for being the best siblings in the world. OJ, my twin cousin and #1 supporter. B for holding me down and having my back. Charles Jr. for always getting me out of jams. S.Dot, always there for me no matter what. Key for teaching me about consciousness and exposing me to what's really going on. Simmons, always pushing me to do better. Armstrong, always seeing the good in me. Schneider, I miss you and love you, so near and dear to my heart. Ms. Clayton, my second mom with that Detroit swagger. P.A.T, my roommate and good friend. Damien, giving me knowledge and a fresh cut. Mikey, never lies to make friends and keeping it a bill. Patrick, always accepting my shortcomings and poor efforts. Ms. Johnson, you always showed me love, regardless. Philadelphia Baptist and Salem Methodist Church for teaching me about good and evil. Fayetteville State for molding me and being the best HBCU school. Carmel Middle School for showing me love and support throughout the years, best school staff in the world. E.T.E.S. for inspiring me to write this book, one of my best working experiences in my life, love you guys. Anointed Cuts for putting up with my foolishness, lol. Meadow View help raise me. Wingate, love my town. Dope dealers who told me not to sell dope. Alcoholics who told me not to be like them. Shooters who told me not to kill others. And anyone who ever helped me, broke bread with me, or said kind words to me... Thanks.

For the angels in the heavens. Paw-Paw, my first role model and loving grandfather, you left me with so much knowledge. Grandma Grace, how you were in your own world with no worries. Hattie Mae, I should have spent more time with you. Sissy, I should of done better.

James Chester always being there for Nuddie. Big Wash, my close friend who taught me about life and people. Chris B, challenging me to get my intellect up, putting me onto new things.

To all my family: The Hueys, the Blakeneys, the Baylarks, the Shannons, the Simpsons, and the Rories. My family is too big to list all their names and titles. I have the best family EVER. They made it possible for me to get through life's ups and downs.

The real shout-out goes to: Mary "Nuddie" Huey. You have always been there for me through your darkest times. You taught me how to view life and treat others with kindness and respect. You always pushed me to do better, how you were able to right your wrongs. Best Mother in the world and galaxy. LOVE YOU!

TABLE OF CONTENTS

INTRO

First and foremost, thanks for purchasing this book, thanks for reading this book, and thanks for giving me a chance to share my knowledge and wisdom with you.

This book is dedicated to Black boys and young Black men as a guide to help them gain knowledge, wisdom, and understanding. This book is like no other. This book is fun, challenging, educational, inspirational, and motivational. There are 100 topics that will enlighten you about life, school, home, church, and much more.

I was inspired to write this book because I felt like so many of our Black boys and young Black men are not getting enough adequate and thorough information from parents, schools, communities, and the government to maximize their full life potential. The more Black boys and young Black men that we can get to reach their full potential, the better their circumstances and situations can improve, the more their communities can thrive. They will possess the ability and power to change laws for equality and be recognized as a positive force in society.

Understand while reading this book, this is just my opinion and my viewpoint of how I see things that can help Black boys and young Black men get through life. I am not guaranteeing your life is going to change overnight or change, period. I will say this, if you're truly looking for change, seeking knowledge, wisdom, and understanding, this book will help with that.

My last thought: this book is coming from the heart. I am not writing this book for financial gain or any notoriety. Even though this book is titled *100 Things Black Boys Should Do and Know*, this is not a racist or race superiority book. In no form or fashion am I trying to down any race, culture, creed, religion, or belief. I am writing this book because we **need** more material, more information for Black boys and young Black men to be exposed to so they can reach the apex of all life options and joys.

THE 100 THINGS

1. Wassup! What's Good?

(GREET OTHERS)

Greet others, whether it's Good morning, Hi, Wassup, or What's good.

The importance of greetings is that others may:

- Think you're nice and approachable

- Be willing to help you in the future

At times, not speaking can be perceived as arrogance or conceit.

There is a saying, "You too good to speak."

2. My Bad

(APOLOGIZE)

Learn and know it's okay to apologize for your mistakes, mishaps, or shortcomings. Sometimes one of the hardest things to do is simply say, "My bad, sorry." Apologizing doesn't make you less than or weak. When you apologize, make sure it's genuine and from the heart, if not, it's not a real apology!

A man who doesn't acknowledge his mistakes is a mistake.

3. Stop Cappin'

(BE TRUTHFUL & HONEST)

Honesty and truthfulness is a trait that takes bravery and integrity and earns others' respect for possessing these qualities.

Some reasons you may be cappin' (lying):

- Avoiding consequences and punishment

- To gain a prize or reward

- Protecting another person from being punished

- To be liked by an individual or group

- Trying to get out of an awkward situation or environment

There are other ways to handle these situations, and I talk about them later.

4. Communication

Communication is the foundation of this world's existence, from Egypt with hieroglyphics to Aztec with prophecies. Communication is vital for asking questions or for help. It's important when talking to your girlfriend or asking your parents for money. I will give you my own principles of positive communication.

- Have good body language, stand up straight, and give eye contact when you're speaking—and listening.

- Make sure your handwriting is legible and as neat as possible so it can be read and understood.

- Use words that you understand and can spell.

- Speak up and clearly so you're understood.

- Know your audience.

And for the love of God, please, *pretty please*, don't shrug your shoulders when someone asks you a question.

5. Tell Your Mom and Dad You Love Them

If you are lucky enough to have them around (or alive), tell your mom and dad you love them as much as possible—even if you're mad at them or they're mad at you. A simple "I LOVE

YOU" can go a long way with that parent, especially if they are having a rough day. None of us are promised tomorrow.

6. Apps You Need

Here are some apps you should download now. They're free! Get to know your community and stay safe.

- Noonlight (Safety)
- Red Panic Button (Safety)
- Zombies, Run! (Exercise/Running)
- Pokémon Go (Exercise/Gaming)
- Nextdoor (Community Events)
- Citizen (Community News)
- ELSA (Pronunciation/Speaking)
- Moovit (Transit)

7. Keep Emergency $

Always keep emergency money on you. Notice I said *emergency*. How much you should keep on you depends on your city, state, country, and age. Keep enough money for food and transportation. Think about how much a fast-food combo costs and how much it is for a couple gallons of gas (or bus transit fare).

8. ID

(IDENTIFICATION)

You need to take ID everywhere, and when I say everywhere, I mean *everywhere*. Keep it in your wallet, bookbag, or pocket. Identification could save your life. When 12 (cops) roll up on you, you can show them your proof of residency and proof that you are a citizen, which could help reduce any police brutality (I cover this later). If you have a medical emergency away from home, they can contact someone from your address or even take you home.

To obtain identification, go to your local DMV (Department of Motor Vehicles). You might need a guardian to assist you with this. The cost is between fifteen to forty dollars depending on the state. You can use school ID if you can't get one from the DMV, but more than likely it won't have your address.

9. Pets

Get a pet if your parents or guardian allow for it! Pets will help you learn responsibility. Some of them will show you unconditional love, and when you feel unsafe, unloved, and unsure of things, they are good to confide in.

10. Words Cut Deep

Be careful what and how you say things to someone—you never know how it might affect someone's life and feelings. Check out an interview Quentin Tarantino did on the podcast "The Moment." It is a deep cut! His mom dissed his writing when he was a kid, so he never gave her a cent when he became successful.

11. You Good

(FORGIVING AND ACCEPTING OTHERS' APOLOGIES)

Another hard thing to do in life is forgiving someone, especially depending on what was done to you. It takes a special and strong individual to forgive and accept others' apologies. Be that special and strong individual to forgive and let them know, "You good."

> "Pay attention to yourselves! If your brother sins, rebuke him, and if he re-
> pents, forgive him, and if he sins against you seven times in the day, and turns
> to you seven times, saying, 'I repent,' you must forgive him." Luke 17:3-4

12. Sink or Swim

Did you know around 70 percent of Black kids do not know how to swim? Some factors why Blacks don't know how to swim are: fear of water, fear of death, no swimming pools in the community, no transportation, or lack of money for lessons. Here are some places to find more information about learning to swim:

- Redcross.org
- Your local aquatic center or YMCA (ymca.org)
- Your school counselor
- Google "free swimming lessons near me"

Did you know that in the UK (United Kingdom) swimming is a part of the national curriculum in primary schools?

13. CPR

Learn CPR! *Learn CPR!* I can't say that enough. After you learn how to swim, you might save your friend from drowning and have to get them breathing again. (You see how I tied that in with "Sink or Swim." LOL.) Real talk, you never know when an emergency might happen to someone you know. Just put your lips on the CPR doll and get certified. Most middle and high schools offer it.

14. Medical ID

If you have severe health issues, get a medical ID in the form of a necklace or bracelet. Health issues you might consider getting a medical ID for include a food allergy, epilepsy, seizures, diabetes, heart condition, physical impairment, or sickle cell. Ask your doctor if they offer a medical ID, if not, ask where you can get one.

15. Don't Litter

Please don't litter. I get it, sometimes throwing down a candy wrapper is no big deal, right? Yes, a very *big* deal. Once people see it, they feel like it's ok to add another candy wrapper, and before you know it... your community is filled with candy wrappers, and now the land owner, city, and county officials can decide to sell or close down your community, forcing you to move out. This sometimes starts gentrification in our communities. Look up gentrification if you need to.

16. Keep a Watch on Your Wrist

This is somewhat old school, but I was told as a kid to always wear a watch, because others will perceive that you have a schedule, value time, and have places to be. You will be amazed how many people will ask you for the time, which will irritate the heck out of you (LOL) but is also a great conversation starter.

17. CPT

(COLOR PEOPLE TIME)

Be on time! *Timing is everything*! There is a stigma that Black people are always late, which is definitely not true. Don't prove it true. Being on time saves time.

18. Friends

All I got to say is to listen to the Dionne Warwick song "That's What Friends Are For." Look it up on YouTube.

19. Don't Just Have Black Friends

Did you know this world has over 650 ethnic groups in over 190 countries with almost 7.8 billion people in total? So yeah, I think you can have more than just Black friends.

20. Brain Break #1

It's important not to overload your brain. Give it a break.

Who's the best hip-hop artist?

    a) J. Cole

    b) 21 Savage

    c) DaBaby

    d) NBA YoungBoy

    e) Lil Durk

21. I Love Music, But

Music does something to our mind, body, and spirit. Music can motivate us to do well and at the same time it can motivate us to do bad. I know a lot of our Black boys listen to hip-hop. Hip-hop is vital and important in our culture, but we just have to be mindful of the hip-hop we listen to. There are a lot of songs rapping about gun violence, killing, drug use, selling drugs, and degrading males and females. You have to ask yourself some questions: Will this influence me in a good or bad way? Can I differentiate between art/expression and reality? Just understand music is very POWERFUL.

22. Bigger than Hip-Hop

Listen to more than hip-hop. Check out some jazz, blues, gospel, and classical. Different genres bring different energy and liveliness to you and your soul.

23. What Are Those

(SHOE GAME)

How many times have you been outside for recess and heard someone say, "What are those?" Shoot, you probably said it yourself or maybe someone said it to you. I get it, sometimes you're just teasing and messing around with others about their shoes. Just understand that kid might not be able to afford other shoes. And eight out of ten times that kid is not going to tell you he or she can't afford other shoes. They will likely cap about how they have more shoes but just like to wear those. So, if a kid tells you to "chill" or "stop saying that," just stop, because that kid might really be affected mentally and emotionally by that.

24. J's on My Feet

There's nothing like J's on your feet. I know right? My favorite J's are the Infrared 6 Jordans. But understand shoes don't make the person or individual. Having J's on your feet doesn't change your personality, your character, or your beliefs.

If you're a jerk, you're just a jerk with J's on.

25. Takis or Hot Cheetos

I will take Takis, especially the Fuego flavor, but Hot Cheetos straight. Just make sure if you eat these, eat them in moderation, don't overconsume. They may affect your health in the short and long term.

Short term: stomach aches, dehydration, nausea, and chest pain

Long term: high blood pressure, high cholesterol, kidney failure, and diabetes

26. Exercise

Exercise is vital for developing your mind and body. Exercise reduces your stress level, lowers your risk of certain diseases, helps with mood swings and anxiety or depression, and can make you feel good about yourself overall. My advice is to exercise or workout something on your body every day. Just playing will do wonders to your body.

27. WATER

You got to drink water! I know how hard it is to drink water as a kid. Trust me! And the temptations are even harder. You're sitting at the cafeteria table, the person on the left is drinking apple juice, the person on the right is drinking a sixteen-ounce cola, and the person in front of you is drinking a cold Hi-C. That's tough, right? Keep drinking your water while the person on the left will have to get a cavity filled, the person on the right will be suffering from severe skin acne, and the person in front of you will be watching their sugar level. This will not necessarily happen, but my point is that water has more positive health benefits than soda and juice. Remember you can always add flavor and get flavored water for a better taste.

28. SHARING IS CARING

Enough has been said about the importance of sharing that I'll just drop some quotes here.

"When someone shares something of value with you and you benefit from it, you have a moral obligation to share it with others." – Chinese proverb

"They who give have all things; they who withhold have nothing."

– Hindu proverb

"One person gives freely, yet gains even more; another withholds unduly, but comes to poverty. A generous person will prosper; whoever refreshes others will be refreshed." – Proverbs 11:24-25

29. LAUGH

Laugh more! Find things that make you laugh. Whether it's a roasting section with you and your friends, watching TikTok, or reading comics. I highly suggest watching *Napoleon Dynamite*. At the end of the day, laugh at yourself, don't take yourself so seriously.

Fun facts: Laughter can reduce heart disease. Fifteen minutes of laughter a day can help you lose weight.

30. Let It Out

(CRY)

As a kid coming up, one of the biggest forms of bullying is being called a "crybaby." I know you have tried to hold and suppress your tears to avoid being called "crybaby." I'm here to say, it's okay to cry. If your feelings are deeply hurt, cry if you need to. If you fall and hurt your knee, it's okay to cry.

I am going to be honest, as a youth, being called a "crybaby" is always going to be around. So make sure you have good friends to lift you up and give you reassurance about yourself. Unfortunately, in the Black community, Black boys are sometimes looked at as weak and less than. We need to stop and break this stigma.

> *Fact*: Crying for a long period of time releases endorphin, which is a chemical in your body to help you be at ease, relax, and get rid of your physical and emotional distress.

31. Get to Know Your Principals and Counselors

I really, really, *really* can't say this enough: Get to know your principal and counselor at your school. This is vital. They have a lot to do with your educational life and future. Principals and counselors can do a lot for you, including:

- Give a recommendation for a job
- Nominate you for awards
- Help you earn a scholarship
- Challenge a discrepancy on your class grade
- Give you options and resources for higher learning and occupational paths

32. Love UR Community

Love your community. Do your part in the community. You might be thinking, "Do what part in the community?" or "I don't know what my part is in the community." Your part can be anything: helping your neighbor with their yard, cleaning up the neighborhood, not doing anything illegal, mentoring kids, starting a book club, not vandalizing property, and the list goes on. You have to ask yourself, "How can I help the community?" And understand it can be the smallest thing that makes a big difference.

33. Join an Organization or Club

I highly recommend you join some kind of organization or club that will make a difference in the world and in your community. If you don't know where to start or how to join one, Google "organizations for kids" or ask your school counselor, your mentor, a community leader, or your parents.

34. Mentor

All Black boys should have a positive mentor. I don't really like Webster's definition of a mentor. For me, a mentor is someone that can influence, advise, and guide you through parts of your life. Anyone you feel is or can be a positive figure in your life can be your mentor. Just ask that person if they would like to be your mentor.

To find a mentor, ask your counselor or community leader, go to organizational events, or go online and search "mentor near me."

35. Ya Mama

"Ya Mama!" How many times have you heard this? Too many times, right? Unfortunately, at times—especially in elementary and some middle schools—this leads to fights. I will role play for you how to combat and limit mama calling and shaming.

Bully J: Ya mama look like a fat Cardi B with no hair.

You: Yeah, you're right.

Bully J: Ya mama got more rolls than tootsie.

You: That's my favorite candy.

You see what I did there? I used the "agree strategy" and then used the "phrase flip strategy." They both work. Once Bully J sees how you're flipping it on them, they will get frustrated and bored. Make sure you don't say anything about their mom though.

36. Fighting

This is a tough one! Not going to lie, there might come a time where you're going to have to fight. But never, *never* go seeking out a fight or trouble. Because one thing I know about a fight is that you never know how it might end. In our community, we sometimes feel like that's how we solve our problem when, in fact, it compounds it. With fighting comes consequences, whether it's ten days of out-of-school suspension, assault charges filed, retaliation, or even death. If all possible, <u>walk away</u>.

37. Self-Defense

Self-defense can help you defend yourself and others. Some self-defense techniques and classes help with confidence, improve health, and teach self-discipline and mediation. Self-defense has to be with our hands, arms, legs, and feet—not with guns, knives, or any other weapon. If possible, seek out self-defense classes or techniques such as Krav Maga, Judo, Muay Thai, and wrestling. Some of these classes are expensive or limited in certain towns and cities. I would *highly* recommend a self-defense class if you can find one near you.

38. Guns

Did you know Black teens and men between the ages of 15 and 34 make up almost 40 percent of gun homicides in the United States? The crazy part is that this demographic makes up just

2 percent of the population. Sit back and think about that. Understand that guns were made for one purpose and that was to KILL. We have to put the guns down. There are other ways to resolve differences and conflicts.

White America knows that within the next fifty years our population will be dwindling, little to nothing. Young Black men are nearly twice as likely to die to gun violence. My challenge to you is to watch the local news for just one week and count how many homicides by guns were done by Black teens and men. You will be amazed!

39. What's Up Slime and Cuz

(GANGS)

I get it, some parts of our society—from rappers, social media influencers, to neighborhoods—are known to glorify gangs. Heck, some of your favorite rappers are gang members. With that being said, for some of you, this will be a defining moment in your life. When you're asked or approached to be in a gang, before you answer, ask yourself:

- Am I willing to die for a color that no one owns?
- Am I willing to die for a flag that's two dollars at Walmart?
- Am I willing to take someone's life?
- Am I willing to serve prison time for the rest of my life?
- Am I willing to put my gang life over my family life?
- What's my life expectancy if I am in a gang?

Being affiliated with gangs in most cities, counties, and states is illegal.

If someone approaches you about being in a gang, check them and ask, "What are the pros and cons about being in your gang?" And if they ask you, "What are pros and cons?" that's your answer right there. Not all people who are in a gang are bad or evil, they are just people who made a bad choice.

40. Brain Break #2

What's your favorite anime?

a) Seven Deadly Sins

b) Hunter x Hunter

c) Dragon Ball Z

d) Naruto

e) Attack on Titan

Give me *Seven Deadly Sins* all day. Meliodas is the truth!

41. Watch Cartoons

Listen, you're a kid, you are supposed to watch cartoons. I know some of your peers try to tease you and say, "I don't watch cartoons, that's for kids." Well, duh! You're a kid, and even if you're not a kid, that's fine too, because I still watch cartoons. I recommend: *Craig of the Creek*, *Phineas and Ferb*, *Tales of Arcadia*, *DuckTales*, and *Kipo and the Age of Wonderbeasts*.

42. Toys R 4 U

Get some toys and play with them. I can't stress this enough: Be a kid. Get your action figures and have them fight each other, get your Hot Wheels cars and make a track, get with your friends to have a Nerf gun shootout. And don't let anyone tell you that you're too big to play with toys. Nowadays, there are many careers dealing with toys. For those who may not have the means for toys, here are some ways to get some for free:

- Websites to become a toy tester

- Local church toy drives, likely during Christmas time

- Websites that allow you to just sign up to send you free toys

- National charity toy drives (Toys for Tots, Boys & Girls Club of America, Stuff-A-Bus, and many others)

43. FORTNITE DOESN'T MEAN ALL NIGHT

(GAMING)

Who doesn't love Fortnite? Who doesn't love gaming? I love gaming! And now you can make serious bank becoming a gamer or a game developer. We all know that gaming can become addictive. That competitive adrenaline we get—having that not giving up mentality—can have a negative effect on your life and health if you game for long periods a day.

Sleep deprivation causes less oxygen to circulate through your brain and body, causing poor judgment and a disconnect with social reality. It can cause you to have poor grades because you put gaming before studying and doing your work. In short, GAME... but don't game all day and all night all the time.

44. GET OUTSIDE

Get off the game system, leave your iPhone in the house. GET OUTSIDE! Yes, I yelled it. Our bodies need to be outside to enjoy nature and get oxygen to our bodies. Appreciate what Mother Nature has supplied us. I don't care if it's going fishing, walking in the park, picking apples from a tree, or building a tree house.

45. LOVE & BASKETBALL, LOVE & FOOTBALL

I know our young Black boys love basketball and football, but there are other sports to love. As a matter of fact, there are over 8,000 sports in the world to love.

I understand your community, city, state, or county might have selective sports, so choices might be limited. Just don't be afraid to try new sports, you never know what new sport you might excel in. In some instances, you might have to leave your friends behind, but other sports might have new friends that look and sound like you!

46. Be a Good Sport

(SPORTSMANSHIP)

A true winner is someone who can show humility when they win and show graciousness when they lose. Guys, I know you're going to talk trash at times during the game and all, just don't make it personal or anything below the belt. And when the game is over, shake hands, hug it out, and let the opponent know that you got respect for them.

But understand this: if you are that sore winner, no one is going to want to shake your hand or hug it out. Main thing about sportsmanship is humility and respect for your opponent.

47. Odds of Being a Professional Athlete

How many times has someone come to your school or your class and asked you and your peers, "Who in here is going to be a professional athlete?" Next thing you know you see 75 percent of your peers (and yourself) raise their hand. Well, that person is probably going to tell you the odds of becoming a professional athlete, which is going to be a crazy, ridiculously low number. I am not going to break down percentages or scenarios of the odds and likelihood of being a professional. All I can say is to listen to that speaker and ask questions. Have a Plan B and a Plan C.

48. Dream vs. Reality

I am all for someone following their dreams. But I am also someone that believes all dreams don't become reality. There are a lot of mantras about dreams. "If you can dream it, you can do it." Or "If you dream it, you can achieve it."

Those quotes are very motivational and inspirational, but is the dream capable of becoming reality physically, mentally, financially, geographically, etc.? Follow your dreams, but follow reality as well.

49. Donate Your Clothes and Toys

Before you throw away your clothes or toys, donate them to someone in the neighborhood, your local community shelter, or post them on any social media platform you are on. Just having that feeling of helping someone is something that cannot be measured or quantified.

50. Nah Bruh

(SLANG)

We sometimes have a habit of using slang all the time, 24/7/365. Know the appropriate time and place and with whom to use slang.

Appropriate: Friends and peers

Not Appropriate: Adults (parents, teachers, police, etc.)

Appropriate: Basketball court, neighborhood, outside

Not Appropriate: Temple, church, household, professional or formal event

Appropriate: Texting, some social media platforms, gaming online

Not Appropriate: Classwork/homework, formal letters, resumes

51. F This, F That

(PROFANITY AND CUSS WORDS)

Cussing doesn't make you big and bad or grown. Typically, it makes you look like someone with a low IQ or a small vocabulary. Even worse, it makes your parents or your guardian look bad because now it's perceived that you have unfit parents. So before you go all *macho* or "Mr. I am 'bout to cuss them out," think about how this is going to reflect on you and your parents and what kind of reputation you want for yourself.

52. You Gay or Dat's Gay

I know some, maybe even most, of guys that say, "You gay" or "Dat's gay" are not deliberately trying to hurt that person's feelings or disrespect the LGBTQ+ community. For the most part, it's used to mean dumb, stupid, crazy, and different.

These phrases really demoralize and minimize people who might be a part of the LGBTQ+ community. When they hear it, it can tremendously affect them, causing serious depression, loneliness, withdrawal, or self-harm. You wouldn't want anyone saying, "You Black" or "Dat's Black," especially coming from another race on top of that. Find another word to replace this. It might not be a big deal to you, but it's a big deal to others.

53. R-Word

I hate even writing this word: "retard" or "retarded." This word should never, I mean *never*, be used. This word is used for hate, belittling, dehumanizing, and degrading someone that you feel superior to. Here is some homework: Ask five people why or why not use the R-word. I will give you two reasons why I don't use it.

The ole folks told us, "You haven't had your kids yet." Meaning: Your kid(s) might look and sound different from "normal kids," hence be called the R-word by others.

Some syndromes and diseases can come later in your life, affecting how you look, how you sound, how you think, and how you walk. Now you're the one being called the R-word. Your mental and physical attributes are never promised.

54. N-Word

Unfortunately, this ugly word will always remain prevalent in our society, whether it's used for endearment, ignorance, hatred, or dismissing. So, you're going to have to always deal with this ugly word, whether it's spelled with an "-er" or "-as."

This is the most complicated word in our society, everybody has their reasons why they do or don't use it. My reason for not using it: too many people have lost their life and continue to lose their life just over this word. Young Black boys and men, as long as we keep using this word to each other, our counterparts are always going to recognize us as such. And news flash, a lot of Black people don't like to be endeared with that word. If you ever see or meet me, endear me with "brother" because I am definitely no "N-word."

55. Ladies First

Have respect for girls and women so they can become fine ladies. Boys and men mentally and emotionally damage girls and women every day of every minute. From calling them B's, thots, and hoes or making fun of their physical appearance.

Speaking of physical appearance, the word "ugly" breaks a young girl's heart all the way down to her soul. Just think how many times you've seen a girl cry because a boy called her ugly. Too many times. Some girls will never be able to recover from this, even when they reach their womanhood. So, we got to uplift our girls and women and especially our Black ones, because they have it hard enough.

There is a saying, "Behind every strong Black man, there is a strong Black woman." We need to help build our Black girls and women up.

56. Sit Down, Be Humble

Sit down, be humble (said in my Kendrick Lamar voice). Listen, be humble with all your accolades, be humble with all your skills and talents, be humble with all your mental and physical possessions. Sit down and let others stand up for you.

Never boast or brag about being better than anyone, no matter the color, race, gender, income, geography, or faith/belief.

"Let someone else praise you, and not your own mouth; an outsider, and not your own lips." – Proverbs 27:2

57. Be Self-Aware

Be self-aware of all your strengths and weaknesses, whether its mental, physical, emotional, spiritual, or financial. Know what makes your strength a strength and your weakness a weakness. Once you understand that, you can enhance your strength and diminish your weakness. If you need help, ask your family and friends what they think your strengths and weaknesses are, and when they tell you, *be humble* and listen. Also, you can talk to a school counselor, mentor, or therapist to help get a better understanding of your strengths and weaknesses.

58. Get Help

(COUNSELING AND THERAPY)

Don't say counseling and therapy around Black boys, you know that's *taboo*. Well, I am going to say it, "Counseling and therapy." This is another hurdle that is hard for our young Black boys to get over. Too many times in the Black community it's looked down on to get mental help, which at times is a trigger for Black boys to not get mental help. Get help, nothing is wrong with that.

When you get help, tell the counselor or therapist everything that's on your mind and in your heart. This will be the time to SPEAK UP so they can help you and get you the help you need. Not going to lie, it's going to be tough to open up about yourself to a stranger, but trust me, it will get better.

All you need to do is go to your school and speak to the counselor and they will guide you to a therapist. Some schools have an in-school therapist. If you don't feel comfortable with a school counselor or therapist, you can always tell your parents you need to talk to someone else. Spiritual places will also have qualified therapists.

59. Get More Help

- ▶ 1-800-422-4453 Childhelp National Child Abuse Hotline (childhelp.org)

- ▶ 1-800-786-2929 National Runaway Safeline (1800runaway.org)

- ▶ 1-800-273-8255 National Suicide Prevention Lifeline
  (suicidepreventionlifeline.org)

- ▶ 1-800-331-9474 National Domestic Violence Hotline (loveisrespect.org)

These helplines will assist you with parental abuse, running away or leaving home, suicidal thoughts or depression, and dating violence. All these helplines are 24/7 whether through call or text. Most also offer an online chat option.

60. Brain Break #3

If you played against LeBron James in a pickup game, playing to seven points, how many points do you think you can score on him if you get the ball first?

My answer is two.

Let me explain. I am going to hit the first shot because I get the ball first, plus he's probably not going to take me seriously and will wait to see if I can shoot. Second point is going to be when he is at six points. He's going to shoot a forty foot shot and miss, and I will run down the rebound and do a quick layup. LOL. That's my strategy, what's yours?

61. Embrace Being Black

Embrace being Black. Like James Brown said, "Say it loud – I'm Black and I'm proud." Black boys and young Black men have so much strength, knowing that every day nothing will be given to us. We get up every day knowing that the world is not fair for us, yet we still persevere. Being Black is having the power to influence people to walk like us, talk like us, dress like us, dance like us, think like us—across the globe. It's mesmerizing!

So don't let any race tell you that you're less than or beneath them. If they were Black for one day, they couldn't survive.

62. My Black Is Better Than Your Black

(COLORISM)

Colorism: prejudice or discrimination against individuals with dark skin tone, typically among people of the same ethnic or racial group (definition from Oxford Languages). This affects our race and community more than any other. This goes back to slavery days. There have been many books by scholars, professors, and intellectuals that explain it in-depth. But whether your complexion is mocha brown or dark chocolate, you're still Black and your complexion doesn't make you better than any other Black complexion.

63. Family Ties

(KNOW YOUR FAMILY LINEAGE AND HISTORY)

It's important for us to learn our family history and know our family lineage. Unlike other races, our families have been divided so many times for so many reasons. It's important to talk to your parents and grandparents. Ask them a million questions. Ask them to tell you stories. Find the oldest statesman or stateswoman in your family and just listen to them talk. Find old pictures and old writings about your family. Go to your family reunion to get to know your third cousin and introduce yourself to as many people as you can. Exchange emails or phone numbers and link up with them on a social media platform.

64. Black History

We should celebrate Black history every day, not just in February or when there is a Black history project due. Right now, places in America are trying to get rid of Black history. As you read this, lawmakers are trying to take Black history out of schools. It's important to do your research on Black history. Purchase or check out Black history books.

It's important to know how you got here, who made it possible for you to have certain rights, liberty, and freedom. So, wake up...

65. HBCUs

I highly recommend you visit and tour HBCUs (Historically Black Colleges and Universities). If you go to some of the schools' websites, they have hours and dates for tours and visits. If you can't tour or visit, go to some HBCU events.

- CIAA Basketball Tournament
- Battle of the Bands
- The Bayou Classic
- The Florida Blue Classic
- HBCU SpringComing

These are just a few. I would highly recommend you ask your parents, older siblings, or a friend's parent to take you to some of these events. Some of the dates and times change. Use this website to keep up with all the upcoming events: eventbrite.com/d/online/hbcu

66. Leave the 'Hood

(TRAVEL)

Travel as much as you can, whether it's going to the next city or town, the nearest state, or overseas. This world is bigger than your 'hood. Explore other lands and destinations. Why should you travel?

- Learn about yourself and others
- Gain a different perspective on life
- Learn about cultural and historical events
- Discover new problem-solving strategies
- Have FUN!

I know some of you might not have the means (money, transportation, and family or friends). So sign up for field trips at your school. Your fees will sometimes be waived if you can't afford it. Churches, temples, mosques, and other spiritual places do a lot of traveling that's free for kids. Joining a club or organization is another way of traveling. See the world!

67. KEEP YOUR HEAD ON THE SWIVEL

(BE AWARE OF YOUR SURROUNDINGS)

Always be alert and aware of your surroundings, no matter where you go or who you are with. Trust your instincts and your Spidey senses. Keep an eye out for something out of place, such as the place is too quiet or the person you're with is acting strange. In this country, we have more drive-by shootings, hate crimes, mass shootings at schools and spiritual places, and kidnapping leading to human trafficking. You have to always keep your head on a swivel, always try to keep in your mind an emergency escape plan, if the situation calls for it.

68. CALL 911

Call 911 if you or someone with you needs medical attention or is in immediate danger or harm. When you call the 911 operator, they typically start off with the same questions. Some of the questions will change based on your response. Questions you may get asked:

- What is the emergency? What happened?
- Where are you? What's your location?
- Who needs help? Who is with you?

If possible, ask your parents or guardian to role play with calling 911 and using situational emergencies or discretion. Practice this every so often. It's going to be hard to simulate emergencies and real emotions but try it anyway.

69. 12

(COPS/POLICE)

If you're a Black boy or Black man, you will have a police encounter at some point in your life, and that is straight facts, homie. I am going to tell you what to do when you get stopped or pulled over by the police.

1) Comply with all instructions and directions given by the officers.
2) Keep your hands in plain sight—DO NOT put them in your pockets.

3) Speak up and use a clear voice.

4) Ask permission for any kind of movement.

5) Give eye contact and use proper body language.

6) Do not use aggressive language or become argumentative.

7) DO NOT RUN!

I know some of the things I listed may go against your values and rights and what you stand for. Understand, your dad and mom just want their son to be alive and well, regardless.

70. Turn Down the Stereo

(STEREOTYPES)

"A stereotype is a fixed, over generalized belief about a particular group or class of people." – Dr. Saul McLeod.

The Black race has more negative stereotypes than any other race. This has been going on since slavery days, used to keep us in place and down. Look up Uncle Tom, Sambo, Coon, Mammy, and Jezebel. Unfortunately, some police, teachers, judges, and elected officials buy into those stereotypes. It causes unlawful arrest, children placed in lower-level classes, unjust verdicts and sentencing, and laws that are bogus and frivolous.

71. Never Ending Race

(RACISM)

Racism will never end in this country or in this world. And that's the Unfortunate Truth. There is always going to be people that hate and discriminate against others because of their race and color. Blacks are the most discriminated people in the world. I mentioned in #66 about traveling, but Blacks will never be able to go to certain places in this world.

You're going to face racism in some form or fashion throughout your life. My advice to you is to pray for their ignorance and hate; if they apologize for their racism forgive them.

Never be racist to anyone no matter what the situation is.

No one can control what color or race they were given at birth. You're going to be in some intense racist situations, but stand up big and strong and let it be known that you will not accept or tolerate racism.

72. Angry Black Boy

(CONTROL ANGER)

It's OK to get angry. It's a very real emotion for everyone. When you get angry, you have to control your anger, someway and somehow. Too many times we let our anger get the best of us, leading to life-changing consequences and life-changing regrets.

When you get angry, don't "hulk out," where you don't think about the pros and cons of what made you mad. Find coping skills that will help you calm down and decompress. And if you get so mad, walk away or leave the situation before you do something or say something that may have severe consequences.

73. Peace Out

(JUST LEAVE)

Anytime you feel like you're in danger or you feel uncomfortable about a situation or environment, just leave. *Always* leave when you see weapons, guns, drugs, and explicit or graphic pictures. Not going to lie, when you do this, some of your peers are going to call you a b*tch, punk, f*ggot, or other derogatory words and phrases. That just lets you know they're not your friends and don't care about your well-being.

That's why I mentioned earlier to have emergency money (#7) and certain apps on your phone (#6) if the need to leave a situation occurs. So, chuck the deuces and peace out!

74. Walk it Out

You might not believe this, but how you walk can tell a person a lot about you. I was taught to "walk like you got business about yourself," meaning walk like you're important or about to do something with importance. Walk with your head up and chest out, and walk with a good pace like you have somewhere to be. People sometimes associate those who walk slow with their head down as a person with nothing to do and nowhere to be. You wouldn't want to walk slow or flap your arms for a job interview, right? Sometimes walking is your first impression on someone, so Walk it Out.

75. Clean Shoes

No dirty shoes, I don't care if your shoes are from Walmart or are Lamelo Ball MB.01 Pumas. Clean your shoes. Another southern country proverb: "Shoes tell you where you been and where you're about to go." Get yourself an old toothbrush, detergent, and two old wash towels. Follow these steps.

1) Remove the shoestrings from each shoe.

2) Fill a cup with eight ounces of water and a small amount of detergent.

3) Dip the toothbrush in the mixture.

4) Scrub only the base of the shoes with the toothbrush.

5) Wipe the base of the shoes with a dry towel.

6) Dip the wash towel into the detergent mixture and ring it out.

7) Use the wet towel to clean the entire shoe.

8) Dry each shoe with a dry wash towel.

9) Put the shoestrings back in.

FYI: This does not work for all shoes and boots; it depends on the material and color for how to clean them.

76. So Fresh, So Clean

(HYGIENE)

Make sure you wash and bathe every day if you have access to water and soap. If you don't have a bathroom or your bath/shower doesn't work, take a "bird bath." What is a "bird bath," you ask? It's when you use just the sink with water in it. Soap up a wash towel and wash your face, underarms, and middle section (front and back)—that's it. It should take you no longer than two minutes. Apply deodorant after every wash. If you have nowhere to bathe or shower, most schools have somewhere you can. Just talk to your principal, counselor, or school social worker. They can provide a wash towel and soap as well.

Make sure you brush your teeth at least once a day to help prevent cavities and keep your teeth white. Believe it or not, some dentists and doctors say unclean teeth is linked to heart disease, dementia, and other diseases. If you need a toothbrush and toothpaste, ask your counselor or school social worker.

If you can, please do both every day. This will create confidence and build self-esteem. If neglected, it will create poor confidence and destroy your self-esteem. A bad hygiene reputation can follow into your adulthood.

77. Dress Appropriately, Appropriately Dress

After you get fresh and clean, it's time to dress appropriately. Whatever the place, venue, event, or destination, always dress the part. Meaning if you're going to school, dress like you're going to school and abide the school dress code. Appropriately dress: make sure your pants are on your waist, your shoes are tied, and your shirt is buttoned correctly.

Disclaimer 1: Please stop wearing hoods when it's like 1,000 degrees outside.

Disclaimer 2: Don't dress nice and have dirty shoes on.

Disclaimer 3: No sagging all the way to your knees.

Disclaimer 4: Wash your clothes once they're dirty.

78. Go See the Doctor

Make sure you go to the doctor for a routine checkup. This will be more on your parents and guardians to take you to the doctor, but you can make sure to remind them that you need to go. For those who have fears and anxiety about the doctor, let me tell you, it will be okay. Use coping strategies to help you with your fears and anxiety toward the doctor. Get reassurance from your parents that things will be alright. Write down any questions and concerns that you might have when visiting the doctor.

79. Shots Shots Shots

(VACCINATIONS)

Shots! Shots! Shots! You will have to get up to around sixteen vaccinations before the age of eighteen. Some will have more shots due to their genetic makeup and health risk. Not going to lie, some shots hurt, but they are needed due to the fact your immune system is weaker and more vulnerable than adults. When you go to get your shots, ask the doctor what kind of vaccinations you're receiving and why. Most schools in America require you to have certain vaccinations to attend. If you don't have them, you might not be eligible to attend until you get them.

80. Brain Break #4

Who would win?

   a) Batman vs. Iron Man

   b) Superman vs. Hulk

   c) Green Lantern vs. Spider-Man

   d) Wonder Woman vs. Captain Marvel

   e) Green Arrow vs. Hawkeye

I got anybody from DC. I am biased. LOL!

81. Donate to Sickle Cell Research

Sickle cell is a red blood cell disorder that is inherited genetically. It's when you don't have enough healthy red blood cells to give your body oxygen, causing extreme fatigue and joint, chest, and abdominal pain. This affects mostly Black people. Most Black families have at least one family member affected by this disease. It's important to donate money, time, blood, and knowledge for sickle cell treatment and research.

Did you know sickle cell funding and research is among the lowest of all major diseases? I wonder why? Take one good guess.

82. Ask Questions

Did you know even a genius asks questions? At times, asking questions can be difficult. These are some reasons why people don't ask questions:

- Insecurities with voice, speech, or appearance
- Lack of confidence
- Fear of the question being dumb and stupid
- Intimidation of the subject, speaker, and audiences
- Taking up time from the person and the group

Some suggestions to help with asking questions:

- Write your questions down on paper and give it to the presenter or group.
- Wait after the session or class to ask questions.
- Email or text the presenter or group, if possible.
- Practice with a friend, teacher, or peer to help you gain confidence.

Ask questions to gain knowledge and understanding.

83. Ask 4 Help

Ask for help any and every time you need it. Never be ashamed to ask for help. We all need help, some more than others. Shoot, I needed help writing this book. LOL. Don't let your pride get in your way in asking for help.

> "Don't be afraid to ask questions. Don't be afraid to ask for help when you need it. I do that every day. Asking for help isn't a sign of weakness, it's a sign of strength. It shows you have the courage to admit when you don't know something, and to learn something new." – Barack Obama

84. Shut Up and Listen

Believe it or not, being a good listener is a talent and skill set. It truly takes practice to become a good listener. It takes superior focus and concentration to listen to what is being said by the presenter(s). When I was in school, our teacher played a listening game with us. The game was simple: a student would be told something by the teacher and the student would have to relay the message to the next student, and that student would relay it to another student and so on and so on. When it got to the last student, the message was never the same as the original message the teacher gave to the first student. Crazy, right? That game showed us what happens with poor communication and poor listening.

Benefits of being a good listener are:

- Save time
- Get things right the first time
- Cut out on mistakes
- Help pass your class and assignment

Sometimes you just have to shut up and listen.

> "When you talk, you are only repeating what you already know. But if you listen, you may learn something new." – Dalai Lama

85. No, No, No

I am going to be completely honest with you. You are going to receive a No more in your life than a Yes. It's a fact. How many times have you asked for video game and the answer was no? How many times have you asked for a new phone the answer was no? How many times have you asked for new shoes and the answer was no? Getting a no is not the end of the world. Actually, a no can help you build and create character. It can help you with perseverance, adversity, and fortitude—to not give up, even when you're told no. Also, there is always a right way and respectable way to have someone change that No into a Yes.

86. Rules Are Rules

Rules are rules, whether you like it or don't like it, whether you think it's stupid or dumb. Rules are typically created for safety, keeping the peace, and fairness. Rules are everywhere, from your house to your school. It's on you to know the rules and follow the rules. And when you break the rules, you have to take responsibility and ownership of any consequences that come with breaking the rules. So, when your parents say, "No gaming after 10:00," and you're gaming at 10:01, don't be upset or angry when your parents take your game system for a week. Rules are going to prepare you for when you become an adult, when rules change into laws.

87. You Did It

(CONSEQUENCES)

Consequences come most times when you break a rule or law. When you break one of these, you have to own it and admit to yourself, "I did it." If you're aware of the rules and laws and you consciously and willingly broke it, you have to be a big boy and deal with the consequences. Don't call for your mom, don't make up an excuse, don't lie or blame someone else. Man up, accept the consequences and deal with it, because you did it.

88. Check In and Update

(CIU)

Check in and update with your parent(s) about what's going on in your life. This is very important. Try to set up a day and time with your parents for CIU, whether it's daily, weekly, or monthly—a day and time *need* to be set up.

And when you have the CIU, be as honest as you possibly can. Express yourself as needed in a respectable way toward your parents. Be able to listen and try to understand when your parents respond to your concerns and questions. Some things they may say might hurt, but you need to have an open heart to know and trust that it's coming from love. CIU can also allow your parents to get you the help you need if you're struggling with drugs, suicidal thoughts, peer pressure, abuse, gangs, or other temptations.

89. R.E.S.P.E.C.T.

People have their own interpretation or perception of what respect is and what respect isn't. You will hear stuff like, "Respect is earned, not given," or "Respect me and I will respect you." My two cents: You first have to respect *yourself* before you even think about someone respecting you. Be a person with standards and uplifting morals and values that will make you and the world a better place and show love and mercy for everyone.

Still, possessing these qualities does not guarantee respect in return. You're going to get disrespected throughout your life journey for different reasons, whether it's because of your skin color, your job title, what kind of shoes you have, and the list goes on. When disrespect comes your way, take the high road, because two wrongs don't make a right. Respect everyone the same way, whether he or she is the janitor or the principal of the school.

90. 10 x 10 = 100 #TBBSDK

(MATH)

Math is everywhere, you can't avoid it. So, with that being said, know and learn math, at least the basics of addition, subtraction, multiplication, and division. Math is always one of the hardest subjects, but practice every day. There are a lot of tips and strategies to become better in math, here are just a few, in no particular order:

- Take good and neat notes in class.

- Ask questions and ask for help.

- Enroll in an online course or program.

- Find a study buddy.

- Download a math app to help solve problems (such as Photomath).

- Maintain a positive mindset.

These tips and strategies can help, but you have to find the tips and strategies that work best for you.

91. %, ¾, 1 Out of 4

(PERCENT, FRACTIONS, PROBABILITIES)

I know some of us do not like math at all. However, make sure you know how to do percentages, fractions, and probabilities. Because in your life, you will deal with these more than any other math. Use some of the tips in #90 to master these too.

92. Read, Read, Read

Read, *read, <u>read</u>*. Seriously! I can't say it enough. Our forefathers fought too hard and died so we can be able to read. Just think about what I just said: they fought too hard and DIED so we can be able to read. Take reading seriously and read every time you have the opportunity. The more we read, the more we know, the more we know, the more we grow.

93. LEARN AND IMPROVE READING

If you don't know how to read or need help improving your reading, it's not too late and you can do it! Know that it's not all your fault for your deficit of reading. It starts with your parents or guardian reading with you before you can even walk. Some research has shown when parents read to their child at an early age, the child will be proficient with reading. If you didn't receive that, you are going to have to put in the work.

Here are some ways to read and improve your reading.

- Use online programs and software

- Access books with subjects you like

- Visit a local library (some have reading classes and reading tutors)

- Watch movies with subtitles

- Get tested for any learning disabilities

There are so many ways to learn and to improve your reading, figure out what works best for you. There are three main things for learning and improving your reading:

1) Parents will need to supply you with technology devices, internet, transportation, and access to books and be an advocate with schools, testing, tutoring, and educational settings.

2) Communicate to your parents, teachers, counselors, and principal that you're struggling with reading so they can help. Be as detailed as you possibly can with why you're struggling.

3) Have a positive mindset that you're going to conquer reading. That means you put in the hard work, be disciplined, put your pride and ego to the side, and don't give up.

94. Tutoring

If you're struggling with anything educational, get a tutor and go to tutoring. Ways and where you can find tutoring, sometimes for free:

- Your local library
- Online sites like understood.org
- Your school teacher or counselor
- Community centers
- A friend or someone in your class

95. Educate Yourself

Learn something every day. Don't depend on the school system or teachers to educate you, because most school systems are broken and outdated. Some teachers are not even qualified. It's important for you to educate yourself so you can seek out the truth, get answers, and gain understanding.

96. You Don't Want that Smoke

(DRUGS/VAPING/WEED/PILLS)

Flat out, don't do drugs—don't vape, don't smoke weed, and don't pop pills. These things will destroy your mind and body, and with your body and brain not fully developed it can cause serious harm. In some states, vaping and smoking weed is legal but you have to be a certain age. Drugs are everywhere, from homes, to schools, to streets, to buses, to bathrooms, to restaurants. Ultimately, it's on you to walk away and say no. There is no one to blame except yourself if you use drugs and become addicted. And I get it, some of your parents and family members use it right in front of you. But say to yourself, "I will not be on drugs like my parents, family, and friends." And if you're around so-called friends that are doing that stuff, they are definitely not your friends.

97. No Bad Energy

No bad energy (said in my Nas voice). It's important for you to bring good energy and leave behind bad energy. I am a big believer in what you put out in the universe will come back to you. If you put out good, positive energy, it will return to you and vice versa: if you put out bad, negative energy it will return as well. My bars:

I have no energy for bad energy,

My energy is a 100. Duracell need more

Than a rabbit to keep up with me. My vibe

Is thermal, kinetic that scientists can't even read.

I got Mother Nature and Father Time saying I'm

Their sun, once I give you this energy the rest is done.

I know, right? That was dope. LOL. Listen, don't worry, I won't quit my day job. But seriously, put out good, positive energy.

98. Prayer and Meditation

It's important for you to pray and meditate every day and whenever you feel the time to. I am a big believer in prayer, I truly believe that prayer changes things. Prayer and meditation help with putting out good, positive energy throughout the day and the universe.

Believe in your prayer and meditation, know that all things you prayed and meditated for will come to existence. Don't let anyone tell you that you're praying wrong, or prayers don't work, or you shouldn't be praying. You pray for those who are saying things like that.

Like MC Hammer said, "We got to pray just to make it today."

99. Spiritual Place

Find yourself a spiritual place, whether it's a church, temple, mosque, or synagogue. These places will guide you through life and help you with your struggles. All these places have resources for everything you might need. No matter what your religion, all have the same foundation about life and humankind. They all practice being kind to one another, helping others, loving everyone, and caring for each other. More often than not, you will feel the good, positive energy at these places.

100. God is Good

God is good, all the time. I am a Christian man, but in no way or form am I trying to belittle or degrad [God Can mean anything to you] God has gotten me through some tough tin [An outside force — (Karma)] his Earth. God hears all my prayers and provi [ ] od in your life, ask someone about him, seek [Some one or Something] ed him more than ever to help us with fake [looking out for you] n violence and laws, drugs, racism, COVID, [ ] My praye [ ] day. Thanks for lding. Protect me from all evil and evil doers. And forgive those who do evil. Give me the strength to overcome every obstacle that comes in front of me, and if I so happen to fall short, know that I will not lose faith in you and your ways.

Please send your angels out for those who are in despair, who are saddened, who have lost all hope and faith. Send your angels to them to let them know that you're the light and the answer and that you will never forsake them or abandon them in their darkest time.

Amen.

OUTRO

Once again, thank you for purchasing and reading and sharing this book. I hope this book has given you the courage, the knowledge, and the understanding of how to accomplish your goals and get the most out of life.

I want everyone, not just Black boys or young Black men, to read this book. I want everyone to be able to help Black boys and Black men: the White parents raising Black boys and Black men, the prominently White schools with a few Black boys, the neighborhoods with just one Black family. This is a good book to try to connect with Black boys and Black young men, a chance to learn about them, get to know some of their issues and concerns, and teach Black boys and young Black men the importance of their existence.

I want this book to be used and read by everyone: the barber breaking it down to the Black youth at the shop; Bible study schooling youth on the topics, blending it in with the Bible lesson; mentors using their weekly check-in time with their mentee to see what they learned from the book and life; after-school programs discussing and dissecting the book; book clubs getting others' viewpoints and opinions; and parents and sons having a healthy, growing relationship while sharing and breaking down the topics of the book.

There will be another book coming soon because I know I left out a lot of things!

Life is always going to be what you make it. Take it upon yourself to make it the best it can possibly be.

Let's love each other and care for each other no matter the color, race, gender, religion, creed, politics, economics, or beliefs.

– Jason "NS" Huey

Made in United States
Troutdale, OR
11/14/2023